BOYS' TOYS

TRAINS

Sourcebooks, Inc.®
Naperville, Illinois

Designer: WDA
Editor: Alison Moss
Researcher: Suzie Green

Sourcebooks, Inc.
P.O. Box 4410, Naperville, Illinois 60567-4410

(630) 961-3900
FAX: (630) 961-2168

Printed and bound in Hong Kong

MQ 10 9 8 7 6 5 4 3 2 1

ISBN: 1-57071-605-6

BOYS' TOYS
4376
TRAINS
HULTON GETTY

1A16
THE
FLYING
SCOTSMAN

INTRODUCTION

From the moment a boy receives his first train set (or manages to persuade his father to let him share his), a lifelong love affair with trains and the railways begins. But what is it about these machines that has so engrossed old and young alike, generation after generation? Is it the romanticism of the steam age, the sheer untamed power of the engines, whose boilers guzzled coal almost as fast it could be shoveled in; the screech of brakes as the locomotives pulled into the railway stations belching smoke; and the chaos at departure time when families and friends waved and kissed their loved ones goodbye? Is it the glorious names—The Flying Scotsman, which traveled nonstop between London and Edinburgh, and the Hiawatha, which dashed between Chicago and Minneapolis?

Steam was replaced by diesel, which in turn was replaced by the streamlined electric trains that can fly like a bullet between destinations. In the beginning they crossed vast continents: now they can travel beneath the sea itself, as the Euro Star from London to Paris has proved. Grown men can still be seen at the smallest of train stations noting down the numbers of trains as they come and go, and even in the jet age, traveling long distance on a train still makes the most jaded of hearts miss a beat.

But it is more than just the trains themselves; it is everything that is bound up with the railways. It is the appreciation of how the system works—the tracks that disappear into the horizon; that meet and cross at the approach to a station; the old signal boxes and the multitude of pulleys and levers to be found within. To work on the railways was every boy's dream. To stand on the footplate of a steam leviathan as it shot through otherwise impenetrable terrain, or hurtled at full speed through a tunnel was also every boy's dream. Even in his later years, any man would gladly give all (well almost all) he owns for a chance to do this. Instead, he buys a toy train set with the excuse that it is for his son, despite the fact that it is kept in the attic, where no one but he is allowed to enter.

The images and quotations in this book will remind us why we love trains so much. All the photographs are taken from the superb Hulton Getty collection and evoke the best of a bygone age. They are sure to entertain those of us who still nurture the secret desire to climb inside one of those huge steam locomotives and drive the train, hearing the hiss and cough of the engine as it works and watching the steam billow out behind; and above all to blow that whistle with its impossibly high pitch.

So sit tight, and enjoy the ride.

“Hudson” locomotive

THE RAILWAY MUST BE IMPOSING,

AND RESPECTABLE,

AND SOLID LOOKING.

NEW YORK
CENTRAL
SYSTEM

INTER-CITY—
THE EASY WAY TO TRAVEL.

WORK IS WHERE YOU FIND IT.

WESTCLOX
CLOCKS
BEN
WESTCLOX
from now on... read New
Sleepercoach

WHY IS IT THAT NOTHING
SEEMS TO KEEP A TRAIN ON
TIME SO MUCH AS YOUR
ARRIVING AT THE STATION
A LITTLE LATE.

Grand Central Station, New York

That train's quite like an old familiar friend.

"Silverlink" locomotive

HAPPINESS IS NOT A STATION YOU ARRIVE AT, BUT A MANNER OF TRAVELING.

WHEN I GROW UP I WANT TO BE A TRAIN DRIVER.

2509
SOUTHEND

WORK IS MUCH MORE FUN THAN FUN.

UPTHRO'
LINE

Signal box room at Liverpool Street Station, London

DO NOT STAND IN A PLACE OF DANGER TRUSTING IN MIRACLES.

RAIL
CROSSING

"Hiawatha" locomotive

HAIL TO THE CHIEF WHO IN TRIUMPH ADVANCES!

2

THE ONLY WAY OF CATCHING A TRAIN I EVER DISCOVERED IS TO MISS THE TRAIN BEFORE.

THE RAILWAYS HAD IN EVERY SENSE A PRESENCE. THEIR VERY APPEARANCE KINDLED A KIND OF AWE AND SENSE OF POETRY THAT SEEMS TO HAVE BEEN SHARED BY PEOPLE OF EVERY CLASS.

PRESS
EUROPEENS
SLEEPING - CAR
I-II CLASS
3790
BOGIE PL 6
D'AXE EN AXE DES ESSIEUX
55500 K.

BAD HABITS ARE LIKE A COMFORTABLE BED.
EASY TO GET INTO BUT HARD TO GET OUT OF.

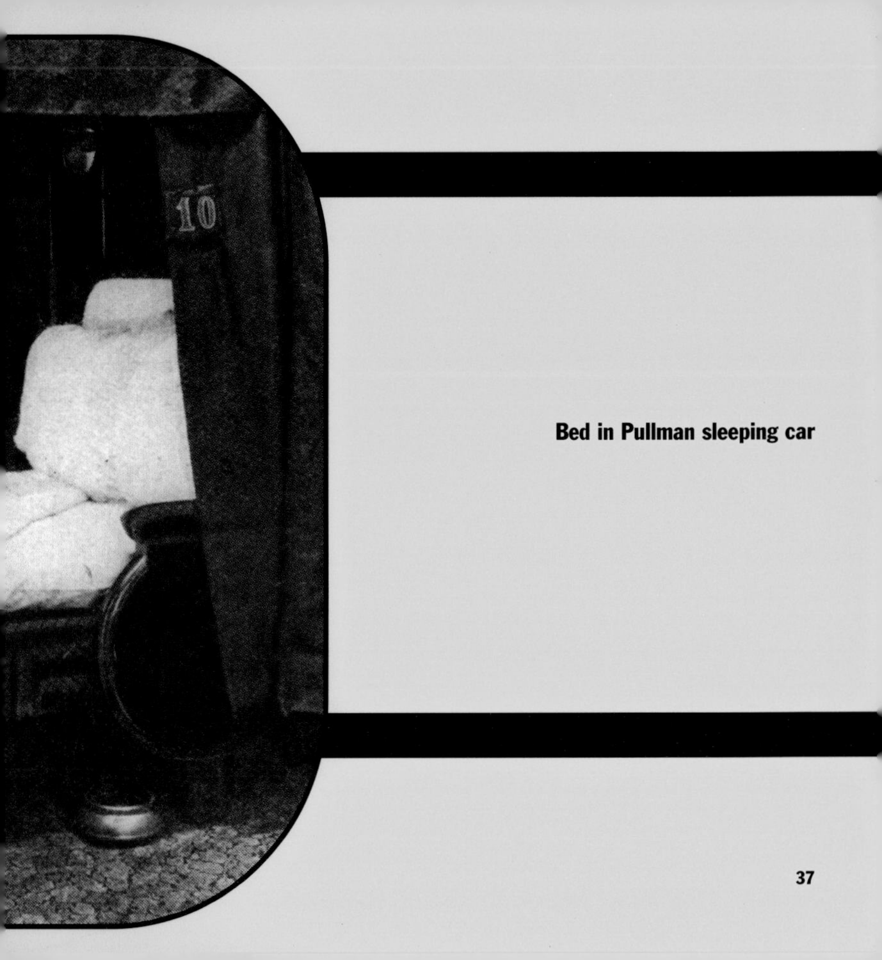

Bed in Pullman sleeping car

If a station is where a train stops what's a work station?

Hobo train

enner

Who hears in the night
The wheels that mutter
Past mill and grave
Past barn and shutter.

Deep chested locomotives whose wheels paw the tracks

LIKE THE HOOVES OF ENORMOUS STEEL HORSES BRIDLED BY TUBING.

-021

The biggest electric train set any boy ever had.

Bullet trains

Model diesel trains

WHEN I WAS A KID, I WENT TO THE STORE AND ASKED THE GUY, "DO YOU HAVE ANY TOY TRAIN SCHEDULES?"

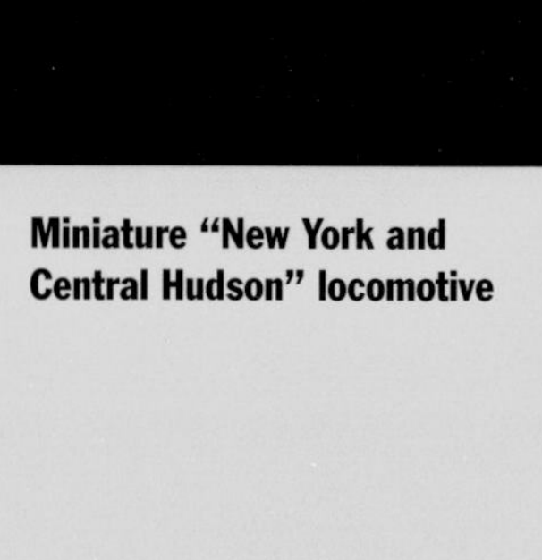

Miniature "New York and Central Hudson" locomotive

N.Y.C.&HRRR

THESE RAILS ALWAYS RUN ONE INTO ANOTHER WITH SLOPING POINTS AND CROSS PASSAGES AND MYSTERIOUS MEANDERING SIDINGS, 'TIL IT SEEMS TO THE THOUGHTFUL STRANGERS TO BE IMPOSSIBLE THAT THE BEST TRAINED ENGINE SHOULD KNOW ITS OWN LINE.

Flying Scotsman express

**UPON THE WHOLE,
THE ADVANTAGES OF A RAIL-ROAD,
ON WHICH LOCOMOTIVE POWER IS USED,
ARE SO STRIKING THAT IT IS A MATTER OF
SURPRISE THIS MODE OF CONVEYANCE HAS
NOT BEEN RESORTED TO EARLIER.**

FLYING
SCOTSMAN

WARNING
DO
NOT
PASS
THIS
SIDE

"Iron horse" commuter train

GOING TO WORK FOR A LARGE COMPANY IS LIKE GETTING ON A TRAIN. ARE YOU GOING SIXTY MILES AN HOUR OR IS THE TRAIN GOING SIXTY MILES AN HOUR AND YOU'RE JUST SITTING STILL.

EVEN IN THE JET AGE, THERE IS A GREATER SENSE OF ADVENTURE AND EXPLORATION IN BOARDING A LONG DISTANCE TRAIN THAN CATCHING A PLANE.

THERE IS A SENSE OF SCALE AND DISTANCE ABOUT A RAILWAY.

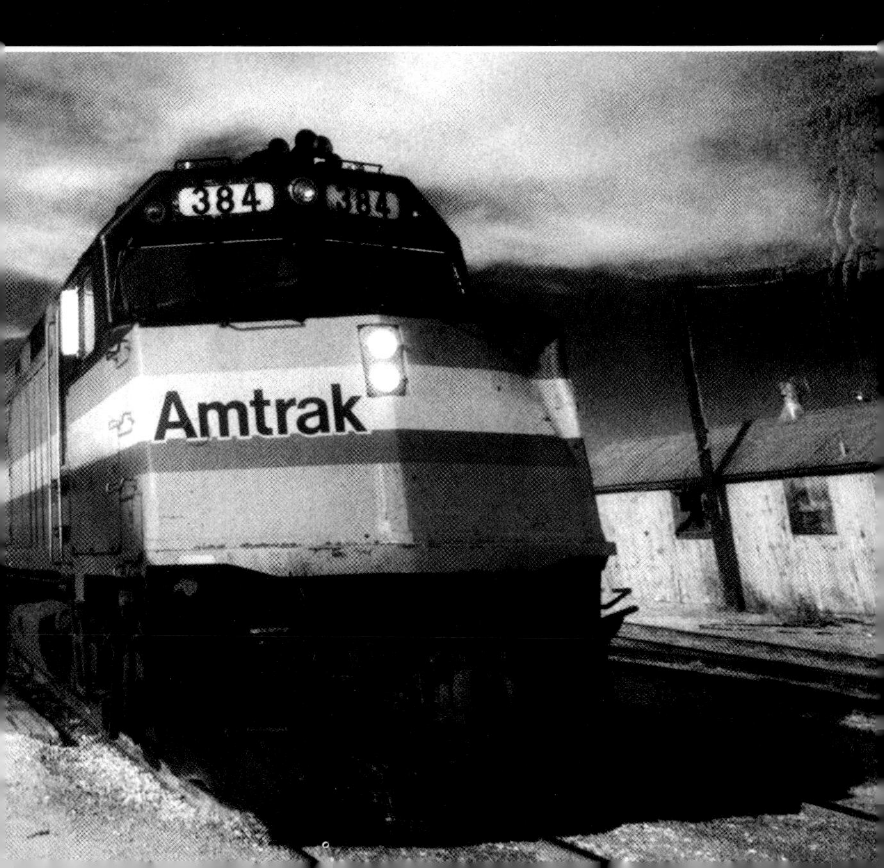

ONE OF THE MOST ENCHANTING CREATURES UNDER HEAVEN.

COCK O' THE NORTH

L N E
2001

YES, BUT DOES IT WORK?

Snow plough

To climb steep hills requires a slow pace at first.

Czechoslovakian mountain train

The train steams in, volleying resplendent clouds of sun-blown vapor.

"Princess Anne"
steam locomotive

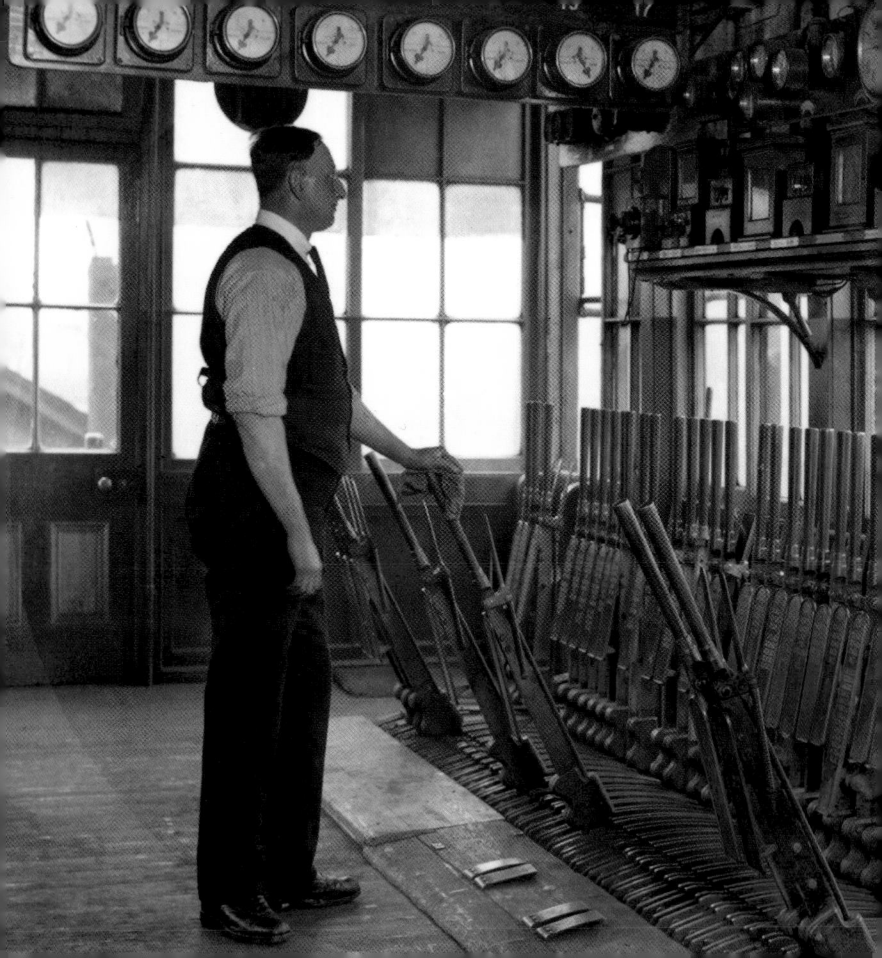

THE LARGE SIGNAL
BOX THAT STANDS
GUARD AT EUSTON.
THIS HIGH HOUSE CONTAINS
MANY LEVERS, STANDING IN
THICK SHINING RANKS.

Office of Western Union train dispatcher, San Augustine, Texas

WESTERN UNION
TELEGRAM

4376

IMAGINATION HAS GIVEN US THE STEAM ENGINE, THE TELEPHONE, THE TALKING MACHINE, AND THE AUTOMOBILE, FOR THESE THINGS HAD TO BE DREAMED OF BEFORE THEY BECAME REALITIES.

An' the Devil says, "Boys, the next stop's Hell"
An' all the passengers yelled with pain
An' begged the Devil to stop the train.

2001

Pendular train

Let the train take the strain.

GANTRY SIGNALS, RUGBY.

YOU CANNOT TELL WHICH WAY THE TRAIN IS COMING BY LOOKING AT THE TRACKS.

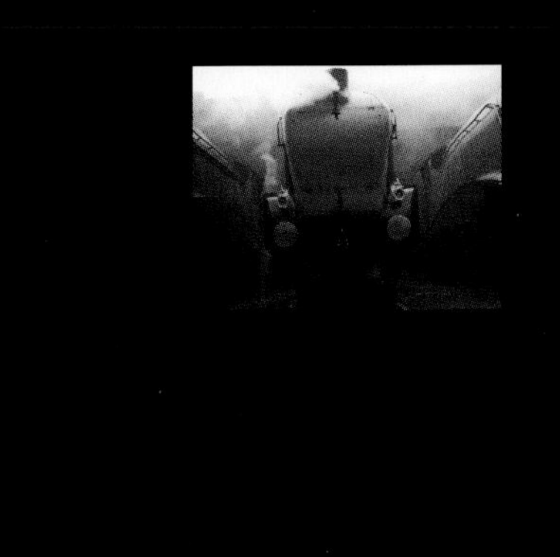

GREATNESS LIES NOT IN BEING STRONG, BUT IN THE RIGHT USE OF STRENGTH.

THE TRAIN RUSHED
OUT OF THE TUNNEL
WITH A SHRIEK AND A SNORT,
AND GLIDED NOISILY PAST THEM.
THEY FELT THE RUSH OF ITS
PASSING, AND THE PEBBLES ON
THE LINE JUMPED AND RATTLED
UNDER IT AS IT WENT BY.

NEITHER A WISE MAN NOR A BRAVE MAN LIES DOWN ON THE TRACKS OF HISTORY TO WAIT FOR THE TRAIN OF THE FUTURE TO RUN OVER HIM.

On the railroad to nowhere.

IT'S OK NOT TO HAVE A TICKET, JUST DON'T GET CAUGHT.

Looking for
KING

Cleveland railway

GOLDEN
ARROW
WILLIAM SHAKESPEARE
4

EVERY ARROW THAT FLIES FEELS THE ATTRACTION OF THE EARTH.

RIDE THE RAILS.

“The City of San Francisco” locomotive

A4 Pacific class "Dominion of New Zealand" Commonwealth train

IF YOU BOARD THE WRONG TRAIN, IT'S
NO USE RUNNING ALONG THE CORRIDOR
IN THE OPPOSITE DIRECTION.

DOMINION OF NEW ZEALAND
Nº 4492

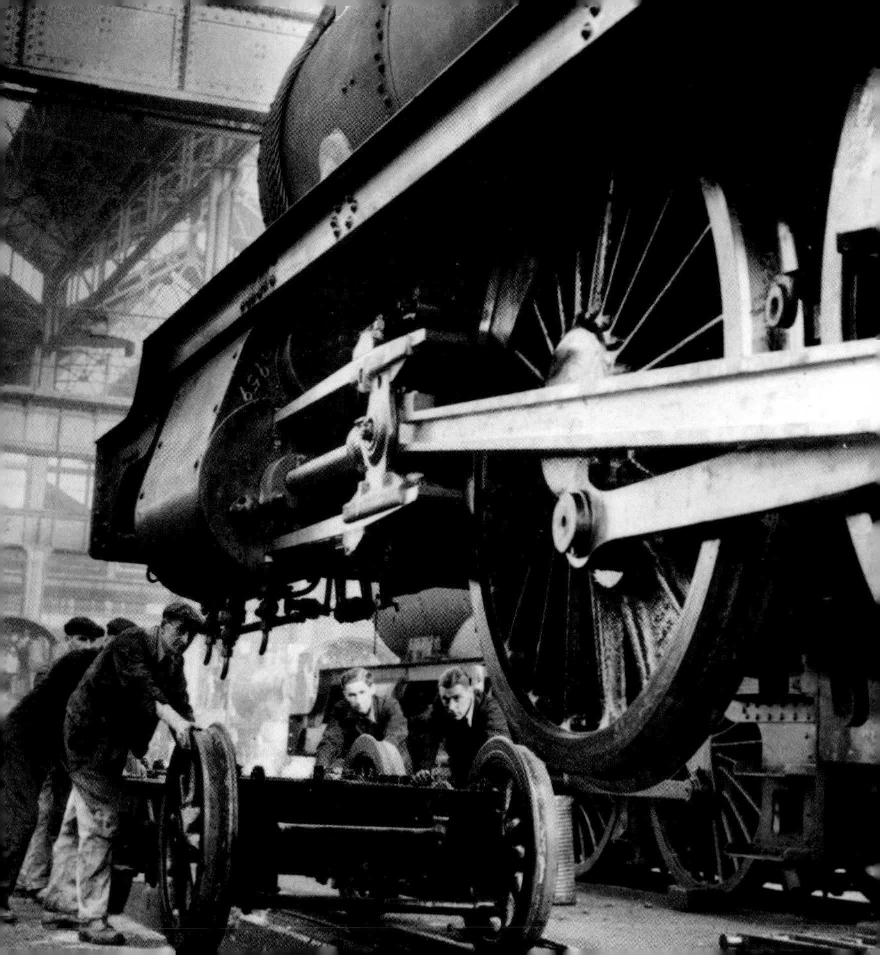

THIS IS A VERY SIMPLE ENGINEERING PROBLEM.

SOUTHERN

NORD

It seems odd to see
all of the train.
It's awfully tall, isn't it?
We always see them cut
in half by platforms.

PICTURE CREDITS

All images Hulton Getty Picture Library

Page 8/9: Steam "Hudson" locomotive on the New York Central Train System, circa 1933.

Page 10/11: Passenger train, 1975.

Page 12/13: Men on a signal gantry on the LNER (London and North Eastern Railway) main line at St Albans Road, Hatfield, 1932.

Page 14/15: American diesel train, 1935.

Page 16/17: Station clock at Grand Central Station, New York, 1965.

Page 18/19: The Flying Scotsman at King's Cross Station, London, being pulled by a new diesel engine, 1962.

Page 20/21: "Silverlink", an LNER engine hauling the Silver Jubilee train of George V, 1935.

Page 22/23: Train driver Bill Perry takes an empty wagon from Willesden to Overseal, 1949.

Page 24/25: Men polishing LMS (London Midland and Scotland) locomotives, 1936.

Page 26/27: The signal box room at Liverpool Street Station, London, 1925.

Page 28/29: Railroad crossing in Las Vegas, Nevada, 1978.

Page 30/31: American locomotive "Hiawatha" which goes from Chicago to Minneapolis, 1936.

Page 32/33: Train departing from Lime Street Station, Liverpool, 1954.

Page 34/35: Railwaymen securing coaches of the Southern Railway Cross Channel train to the deck of the ferry, 1936.

Page 36/37: Bed in the luxury Pullman sleeping car, circa 1880.

Page 38/39: A hobo shows his membership card before boarding a freight train, circa 1955.

Page 40/41: Coal train on the Brenner Pass, between Germany and Italy, circa 1940.

Page 42/43: LNER locomotives during a performance test in London, 1937.

Page 44/45: Japanese electric bullet trains, 1964.

Page 46/47: Model diesel trains emerging from repair yards, circa 1955.

Page 48/49: Miniature "New York and Central Hudson" locomotive.

Page 50/51: Railway tracks and semaphore signals at Boston, Massachusetts, circa 1946.

Page 52/53: "Hush Hush" LNER engine hauling the Flying Scotsman express out of King's Cross Station, London, 1930.

Page 54/55: Commuters boarding the train, circa 1955.

Page 56/57: Amtrak railway train, circa 1970.
Page 58/59: 150-ton Flying Scotsman LNER "Pacific" locomotive alongside the 8-ton "Typhoon" of the RHD (Romney, Hythe and Dymchurch) light railway, 1927.
Page 60/61: LNER's "Cock of the North" on the turntable at King's Cross Station, London, circa 1934.
Page 62/63: Thomas Hornsby, Divisional General Manager of the LNER showing Sir Murrough J. Wilson the latest design in the railway snow ploughs at an exhibition of rolling stock at Darlington Station, 1928.
Page 64/65: Electric train which joins Strbske Pleso with Tatranska Lomince in the Tatra Mountains, Czechoslovakia, circa 1950.
Pages 66/67: Steam locomotive "Princess Anne" at Camden, London, beside LNWR (London North-Western Railway) lower quadrant signals, 1952.
Page 68/69: Signal box at King's Cross Station, London, 1925.
Page 70/71: Office of the Western Union train dispatcher at San Augustine, Texas, 1939.
Page 72/73: Saturday morning train taking New Yorkers to the countryside, circa 1955.
Page 74/75: Steam train crosses the Firth of Forth railway bridge, circa 1930.
Page 76/77: Pendular railway train at Gare de Lyon station, Paris, 1964.
Page 78/79: Experimental train carriage with reclining seats on the Pennsylvania railroad.
Page 80/81: Gantry signals at Rugby, circa 1970.
Page 82/83: "Royal Scot" steam train in action, 1933.
Page 84/85: Steam locomotives in sidings, circa 1950.
Page 86/87: Steam locomotive entering a tunnel on the Flute Line, which passes through the Peak District between Derby and Manchester, 1936.
Page 88/89: Shunter checking his train at Hither Green Station, London, 1948.
Page 90/91: Water tower alongside the track in Jennings, Maryland, 1937.
Page 92/93: Philadelphia-bound train, circa 1958.
Page 94/95: Train arriving at a station in Cleveland, Ohio, circa 1950.
Page 96/97: Steam locomotive "Golden Arrow", circa 1930.
Page 98/99: "The City of San Francisco" locomotive which travels between Chicago and San Francisco, 1936.
Page 100/101: A4 Pacific class train "Dominion of New Zealand" leaving King's Cross Station, London, 1938.
Page 102/103: GWR (Great Western Railway) locomotive has her bogie wheels replaced, 1937.
Page 104/105: "Channel Packet" engine on a trial run from its yard, circa 1941.
Page 106/107: Steam locomotive at Gare du Nord station, Paris, 1929.

ATTRIBUTIONS

Page 8/9: Hamilton Ellis.

Page 10/11: British Rail ad.

Page 12/13: Anon.

Page 16/17: Anon.

Page 18/19: Siegfried Sassoon.

Page 20/21: Margaret Lee Runbeck.

Page 22/23: Anon.

Page 24/25: Noel Coward.

Page 28/29: Dwight D. Eisenhower.

Page 30/31: Sir Walter Scott.

Page 32/33: G. K. Chesterton.

Page 34/35: Dyos & Aldcroft.

Page 36/37: Anon.

Page 38/39: Anon.

Page 40/41: Elizabeth Richmond Riddell from "The Train in the Night."

Page 42/43: T. F. Marinetti.

Page 44/45: Orson Welles.

Page 46/47: Steven Wright.

Page 50/51: A. Trollop.

Page 52/53: Charles Lawrence.

Page 54/55: J. Paul Getty.

Page 56/57: Trevor Fishlock.

Page 58/59: Joseph Locke.

Page 62/63: Anon.

Page 64/65: William Shakespeare.

Page 66/67: Siegfried Sassoon.

Page 68/69: Stemphe Crane.

Page 72/73: L. Frank Baum.

Page 74/75: J. W. Pruitt. from "The Hell Bound Train."

Page 76/77: Anon.

Page 78/79: Anon.

Page 80/81: Mike Ingram.

Page 84/85: Henry Ward Beecher.

Page 86/87: Phyllis in *The Railway Children* by E. Nesbit.

Page 88/89: Arabian Proverb.

Page 90/91: Anon.

Page 92/93: Anon.

Page 96/97: Henry Wadsworth Longfellow.

Page 98/99: To travel by rail without a ticket.

Page 100/101: Dietrich Bonhoeffer.

Page 102/103: Howard Hughes.

Page 106/107: Phyllis in *The Railway Children* by E. Nesbit.

Excerpt by Hamilton Ellis used with permission from *Steam Railways* by Hamilton Ellis, published in 1975 by Methuen.

Excerpt by Trevor Fishlock used with permission from *Americans and Nothing Else* by Trevor Fishlock, published in 1980 by Cassell & Co.